DILIGENCE

noun | **dil-i-gence**

careful and persistent work or effort

Dedication

To my mother, Kathleen, who is the most humble and resilient person I have ever known. Thank you for shaping me to be the man I am today. You are very much appreciated.

Acknowledgements

First and foremost, I want to thank my Lord and Savior Jesus Christ for his   continued patience with me and for blessing me with the idea and storyline for this book.

To the Godfather, YouTuber, and image consultant, Kevin Samuels. Thank you for inspiring me to pursue my commercial driver's license and for sharing your wisdom on your platform. You are heavily contributing to making this world a better place.

Thank you, Delorean Andrews for sharing your wealth of knowledge with me on the stock market. I will always be grateful for our coaching calls, as they taught me a lot. Many others could also learn a thing or two from you.

Vince Hollerman, a.k.a. Coach Vince, who consistently teaches about money and mindset on social media. I appreciate you educating myself and others on trading options; another asset to our community.

Thank you to my outstanding publishing team for the professionalism, not to mention excellence in putting this book together. Thank you for making the   publishing process a smooth one for me, Mrs. Julia.

A special thanks to my pastor, Alvin Motley of The Way Thru Christ Community Fellowship, for being like a father to me, and showing a great example as a man of God.

Introduction

This book was written from inspiration after watching Larry Jones on his YouTube channel, STOCK UP! with LARRY JONES. In one particular video, he was discussing an exchange traded fund (ETF) that had a high rate of return over a period of five years. "This isn't the kind of information you typically learn in school," I thought to myself. In fact, I wish I started investing in an ETF when I was a teenager. I finally realized it is better to start investing at a young age because wealth grows over time (Proverbs 13:11 NLT).

Now, I share this inspiration with you through the example of the main character in this book, Lamont.

Lamont was 13 years old when he was walking by a shoe store with his father. He tugged his father's arm and said, "Dad, those are the new kicks I was telling you about! Can I buy them?"

"Look at the price," said Lamont's father, "They cost $300!"

"Do you have that much money?" asked his father.

"No, I only have $100," said Lamont.

"So, you're willing to spend all of your allowance, plus another $200 you don't have on some sneakers?"

3

Lamont had a sad look on his face. "Come on son. Let me explain what you should do with your $100," his father said as they walked away.

During lunchtime at school, there were a group of boys named Corey, Calvin, and Rick sitting together in the cafeteria. Lamont attempted to sit with them. Before he could sit down, Corey rudely said, "No, Lamont, you're not sitting here. Leave!"

"Why?" asked Lamont.

"Look what you're wearing. Your clothes look so cheap!" said Corey. Calvin and Rick started giggling.

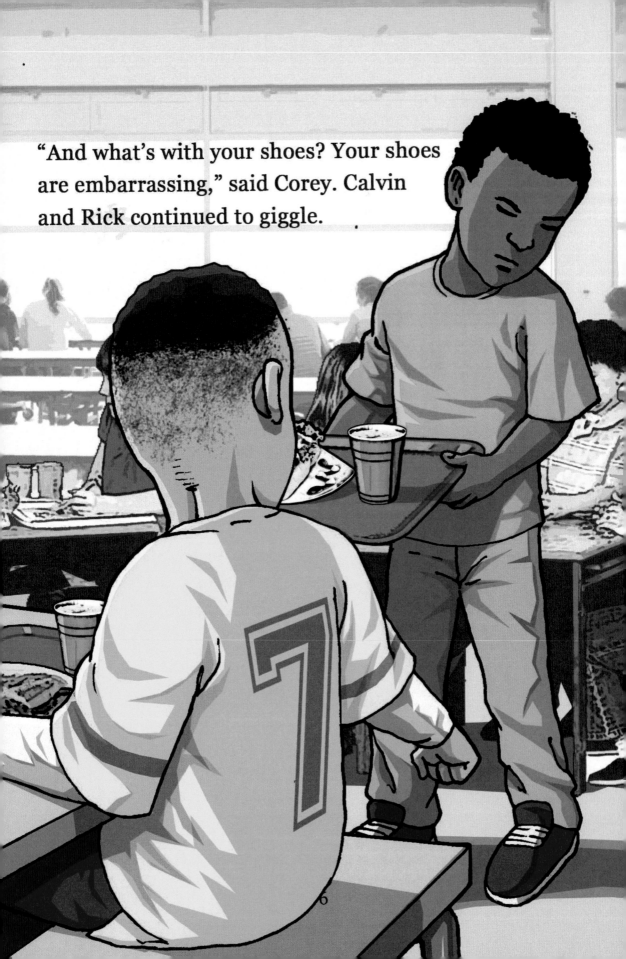

"And what's with your shoes? Your shoes are embarrassing," said Corey. Calvin and Rick continued to giggle.

6

"I'm trying not to spend much money on clothes, so I can save more" explained Lamont. Before he could continue explaining why he was saving his money, Corey cut him off and said, "Man, who cares." He then pointed his thumb and said, "Go sit somewhere else." Lamont took a deep breath and walked away with his lunch.

After school, Lamont was mowing the lawn in his backyard as part of his allowance.

His father showed him how to trim the
edges of the front lawn.

The next day after school, Lamont was mowing the lawn and trimming the edges of the grass for a neighbor. The neighbor thanked Lamont by paying him in cash.

Lamont went to another neighbor with his lawn equipment, cut their grass, and received another cash payment.

Then, he repeated for another neighbor, who paid him through an app called Cash Me.

It was another nice day outside when Lamont noticed a car in front of a neighbor's house that appeared to be dirty. He asked his mother if he could wash the car to make some more money. His mother smiled and said, "As long as it's okay with the owner of the car. Let's go to the house and ask."

Lamont and his mother rang the doorbell. A woman answered the door. Lamont's mother introduced herself and her son and proceeded to ask if her son could wash the car for her. The woman was delighted and accepted the offer.

Lamont's mother and the woman sat on the doorstep together, while Lamont washed the car. The woman thanked Lamont by paying him in cash before he returned home with his mother.

One day Corey, Calvin, and Rick were walking along a shopping strip wearing expensive clothes. They were each carrying bags filled with more expensive clothing that they just bought.

As they approached a thrift store, they saw Lamont walking out, carrying his shopping bags. They began to make fun of him. "Man, why are you shopping at a thrift store?" asked Calvin.

"You need to be getting the kind of clothes we got," said Rick.

"I'm living on a budget," said Lamont. Corey, Calvin, and Rick looked at each other, then looked at Lamont like he was weird. "You see, I've been working to earn some money, so I can invest $100 a month in an ETF."

"A what?!" said Corey, mocking Lamont. The three of them continued to laugh at Lamont before he could finish explaining himself. "Come on, y'all. Let's get away from this geek," said Corey. They proceeded to walk away, as Lamont took a deep breath to calm his nerves.

Lamont, now 14 years old, was in high school, acing his math classes. Math was his favorite subject. He always received an A on every homework assignment and test.

19

One day he noticed a student named Amy who didn't do very well on a test. Lamont offered his tutoring services to her and she accepted.

20

Lamont, Amy, and her mother were in the school library, having a tutoring session. They were working on algebra together.

The following week, Lamont's algebra class had another test. Lamont got his usual A...

...and this time, Amy got a B+ on her test!

Amy's mother thanked Lamont for his help by sending $50 to his Cash Me account.

On another nice day, Lamont was dog walking for a man in his neighborhood. When he returned the dog, the man gave him a cash payment.

25

Soon wintertime arrived and there was a lot of snow on the ground. Lamont saw this as an opportunity to shovel the driveways of his neighbors for a fee. He removed the snow from the cars and the front doors of as many houses as he could. Everyone he shoveled for either paid him in cash or through Cash Me.

Month after month, without any excuses, Lamont consistently found a way to earn a total of $100. He would then give the money to his father by the end of each month, who would put the money in the ETF for him.

Lamont, now 16 years old, had a job working as a cashier at a supermarket. He would go to his job almost every day after school.

As Lamont received a paycheck for his work from the supermarket, he would deposit the check into his savings account.

He always made sure to set $100 aside to give to his father at the end of each month. His father would put the money in the ETF for him. Lamont consistently used his job to earn the $100 he needed to give to his father every month, without any excuses.

Lamont, now 18 years old, had a car. He no longer worked at the supermarket. He used his car and his smartphone to deliver food for a living. He has been investing $100 in the ETF on his own now that he was 18.

Lamont, now 21 years old, received an order on his phone. He accepted the order, picked up the food from the restaurant, and drove off.

As Lamont drove closer to the customer, he saw that it was Corey, waiting outside his apartment for the food to be delivered.

Lamont stepped outside of his car to hand him his food, only for Corey to laugh at his car. "What's so funny?" asked Lamont.

"This is your car? What a piece of junk!" said Corey.

"Well, where's your car?" asked Lamont.

Corey pulled out his car remote, which unlocked an expensive car nearby. "That's my new ride," he said arrogantly as he pointed to his car.

"Wow, that is a nice car," said Lamont. "What's the payment on it?" he asked.

"I don't know, and I don't care, because she looks so good! And I plan on driving her to the club tonight," said Corey.

"Well, have fun," said Lamont. "I'm just going to keep delivering until I earn my $100. Here's your food." Lamont handed Corey his food, then drove off.

Corey had a strange look on his face. He remembered Lamont saying something about $100 when they were at the thrift store several years ago.

But Corey still went partying at the club that night. He was popping champagne bottles and spending all the money he had. Corey was acting like he was rich, attempting to impress the people around him.

Lamont, on the other hand, continued to deliver food with his car and invested the money he was earning every month into the ETF.

ne morning, Corey, now 35 years old, was walking
ward a bagel shop across the street from his apart-
ent. He was wearing an old pair of jeans and a
shirt.

Suddenly, a very expensive luxury car pulled up and parked in front of the bagel shop.

When the door opened, Corey was surprised to see someone he recognized getting out of the car.

It was Lamont! Also 35 years old, and wearing a very nice, tailored suit.

Before Lamont could enter the bagel shop, Corey said to him, "Lamont?"

"Corey? Hey, man, it's been a while," said Lamont.

"Yeah, it has," said Corey. "Wow is this your car?" he asked with a surprised tone.

"Yeah, I bought it last week," said Lamont, as he locked it with his remote.

"Wow... what's the payment on it?" asked Corey.

Lamont laughed and said, "Payment? I paid cash for it." Corey had a dumbfounded look on his face.

"Where's your car?" he asked Corey.

"Oh," Corey chuckled. "My car got repossessed because I couldn't afford the payments anymore. That's why I'm walking."

Lamont shook his head with shame.

"How can you afford this car?" asked Corey.

"Okay, check this out," said Lamont.

"Ever since we were 13 years old, I've been investing $100 a month in an ETF, otherwise known as an Exchange Traded Fund. My father got me started with that. He taught me to pay myself first, and spend later."

Lamont continued, "While you were spending your money on clothes, shoes, and cars you couldn't afford, I was working to build an emergency fund and invest $100 consistently every month into an ETF. This ETF had been doing well over the last 22 years, it's made me a multi-millionaire."

Corey once again had a dumbfounded look on his face.

"You see, I used to think just like you," Lamont continued. "When we were 13, I wanted to buy some shoes I couldn't afford, but my father stopped me and told me to start saving my money. He taught me to invest $100 every month into the ETF so I could be a millionaire by my 30's... and it worked!" said Lamont.

"Now it all makes sense," said Corey. "That's why you said you were trying to earn $100 when you delivered my food," said Corey as he pointed to his apartment. The same apartment Lamont delivered Corey's food to all those years ago.

"That's right. I tried to explain this to you when we were kids, but you laughed at me and called me a geek instead of listening," said Lamont.

Corey had a shameful look on his face as he apologized to Lamont.

43

"It's all good. I forgive you," said Lamont.

"Do you think you could teach me how to build wealth sometime?" asked Corey.

Lamont agreed and said, "Sure, I'll help you, but I charge $100 for an hour of advice."

Corey was so inspired, he agreed to Lamont's services. Lamont reached his hand out appearing to want a handshake. Corey shook his hand, but Lamont responded, "I don't want your hand, I want my $100."

"Oh, I'm sorry. I'll run to my apartment and get the money," said Corey. When Corey took off running, Lamont laughed and said, "I was just playing. You can just Cash Me when you're ready to book a session." Corey laughed with him and said, "That was a good one. I deserved that."

"Well, I have to get inside. I have a meeting with my property manager," said Lamont.

"Property manager?" asked Corey in another surprised tone. "For what property?"

"The one you're living in," said Lamont as he went into the bagel shop.

An exchange-traded fund (ETF) is a basket of stocks you buy or sell through a brokerage firm on a stock exchange.

If you are 13 years old and invest only $100 a month in an ETF earning 35% per year.

Your net worth could estimate $3 million by the age of 35.

You'd be able to retire early, since most people retire in their 50s and 60s.

https://www.calculator.net/investment-calculator.html

"Plans go wrong for lack of advice; many advisers bring success."

Proverbs 15:22 NLT